the key:

lady grizzly & sir charles otter

Also by Ice Gayle Johnson

A Cautionary Tale: Peer into the Lives of Seven New York Performing Poets (New York: Uphook Press, 2008), editor with Theo Coates, Pete Dolack, Bob Hart

you say. say. (New York: Uphook Press, 2009), editor with Jane Ormerod, Brant Lyon

Hell Strung and Crooked (New York: Uphook Press, 2010), editor with Jane Ormerod, Brant Lyon, Thomas Fucaloro

gape-seed (New York: Uphook Press, 2011), editor with Jane Ormerod, Brant Lyon, Thomas Fucaloro

the key:
lady grizzly & sir charles otter

ICE GAYLE JOHNSON

POETS WEAR PRADA • Hoboken, New Jersey

The Key: Lady Grizzly & Sir Charles Otter

First North American Publication 2012

Poets Wear Prada, 533 Bloomfield Street, 2nd Floor, Hoboken, NJ 07030
http://pwpbooks.blogspot.com/

Grateful acknowledgment is made to the following publications where some of these poems have or are scheduled to appear:

First Literary Review – East; Poetry in Performance, 33 (City College of New York/CUNY Press, 2005); Poetry in Performance, 38 (City College of New York/CUNY Press, 2010); Spiny Babbler Arts of Kathmandu Anthology, eds. Brant Lyon & Liza Wolsky (Spiny Babbler, 2012).

ISBN-13: 978-0615606514
ISBN-10: 0615606512

Printed in the U.S.A.

Front cover photo: Ice Gayle Johnson
Author photo: Ice Gayle Johnson

tillie & charlie

Table of Contents

the key:

lady grizzly & sir charles otter

The Key

When I leave I keep the key
I don't want to live there
I don't want to listen to "you did *this* and *this*"
"Whore" and more

I keep the key
Sometimes late at night I sneak in
My mother never says: "stay another day"

I keep the key
Late at night at the kitchen table
Chattering between he and she
I open the door walk past them
We don't speak

In the morning she doesn't wake me
She goes downstairs
And puts money in the meter
So I won't get a ticket

I keep the key
I keep the key
I
keep the key

Cement

Here I am with my feet stuck in cement
My feet stuck in a bucket again

I don't know how I manage this —
I can't move my legs:

I can lean forward
I can lean backward
I can sway to the left and the right
I can move my hips in time to the music

If I could only feel a slight movement
Possibly a tiny crack in the cement

Morning comes

Night dims and turns out the light
It's all on a timer

Dear God if you can hear me
Are you the one?

Are
     you
          the
               one?

Fragments
Inspired by Nick Flynn

They always show up unannounced —

1.

Army pants hang on a hook in the bathroom
Over his shirt belt and jacket
His combat boots stand side by side
While he sleeps
I often help myself to loose change in his pockets

2.

He works nights and she works days
They are never home together, except one day a week
Today — they're going to the movies!

Hysterical I sit outside in the hall, firmly attached to the bars of the handrail
I stay there until my father comes home, leaving her alone in the theater
He says my *hysteria* rings in his head — impossible for him to leave me

Later she comes home yanks me out of his arms screams
"Why can't I have one night alone with my husband — *without* you!"

I wear slapping hands to bed

3.

"Get away! get away! I only love Marilyn — when I beat her up
She listens to me — you, you! I can beat you up ten times a day
And you do exactly what you want   so get away from me
I don't love you anymore!"

4.

In the hallway on the landing below the third floor where we live
I sleep with my left arm tucked in my lap   so stiff from
Slamming the dresser drawer   (the drawer is cracked in half)
My arm could be broken   I was looking for my new lingerie

I ask my mother: "did you see my new lingerie?"

She says no, but I *know*   when she *lies*

I say: "you gave it to Marilyn didn't you   you did you did   you love her
More than you love me, I know you do"

My mother says: "you're right   yes, I do   I don't know why
maybe it's because *she*'s my firstborn"

5.

It's Saturday, we always go shopping downtown, first we shop at
Lane Bryant, it's a shop for the *full-figured* woman — mother maybe is 5 ft 2
And for as long as I can remember, she has weighed 215 lbs

6.

My sister catches me coming out of the church

I hide there after school

I watch the nuns they scare me they intrigue me
They seem to float when they walk
They're so mysterious, they have an angel-like look

I wanna be a nun

"Ooh!!! I'm going to tell mommy and daddy on you!"
My sister threatens me blackmails me into doing all kinds of things
Otherwise she'll spill the beans

Finally after a day or two I say: "go ahead you bitch and then I'll

I'll cut up   all your clothes!"

My father tells me not to go there, and shares his story of how he escaped the Nazis:
"If the priest finds you he'll keep you he won't let you come home,
He'll take you downstairs to the basement bury you there,
Just like they did me"

7.
When I was fifteen it was a mighty good year:
A world opens without slapping hands flying plates silverware
Random objects

One last time we see each other in a room
It's a sterile all-white room

"I know you and I have never been friends
I want you to know I've always admired you
You're so strong so determined never let anything stop you
I could never be or do any of those things"

8.
The room was full of chattering: they whisper to each other as I pass
Dressed all in black I sit in the front row where the family sits
The casket is open   I walk up to see if her hair and make-up still look good
I put the palm of my hand under her ice-cold head — it drops hard!

In the director's office on the couch with a cold towel on my forehead
I open my eyes —
My uncle says: "what were you thinking?"

9.
She shows up in summer in the morning in the afternoon   late at night
Especially when I write
Then the both of you show up unannounced:
The dead should be more respectful   you two should know your place

Army Fatigues

On the hook inside the bathroom door
My father's army fatigues hang
Often I help lighten the bulk of change in his pockets
While he sleeps

Sometimes I prop his hat on my head
Tuck all my hair inside
Pull it down over my eyebrows
Button his shirt
Buckle his pants tight around my waist
Tuck the pants inside his boots
Flip-flop around the house

Swallowed up in combat clothes
Laughter paints the walls
I love to wear his clothes smell his body over mine
Run around the house
Make everyone laugh
I'm a *silly bum* a mime

My father laughs   I laugh harder
I take his shopping bag
With his lunch, his book, his bottle of whiskey
Pretend I'm going to work to clean and mop the laundry

When my father comes from Vilnius a death camp during the war
His friend gives him a job   (it's a piece of war history)
My father's brothers and sisters flee to South Africa
He's separated from them for more than ten years   they live in California
We were never friends   (I never understood any of this)

He and his friend   they both escaped the Nazis

Army Man

1.

I see him off in the distance
Hey, wait for me!
I wave and run at the same time
He's almost inside the train station
When he sees me
His combat boots, army fatigues,
Jacket and hat all fit together
He carries a shopping bag
In it his lunch, a book, a bottle of whiskey
He's a night watchman for a friend
Who comes from Vilnius
He escaped the Nazis too   just like my father
Daddy daddy, wait, take me with you!

2.

He always wears
An army shirt
His hat, army fatigues, combat boots,
I don't remember him dressing in any other clothes
I never question
I never think this is not normal
I never ever think to ask why people   why people think he's my grandfather
I never think to ask why he cleans a laundry for his friend
I never ask why he writes in a language I don't know
I never ask where and why his family are people I don't know
I did go to California to try and meet some of my aunts and uncles
I did question why everyone was so much older than I
I did question why we didn't know them
I leave without answers

3.

At the kitchen table early in the morning
He sleeps with his pipe hanging from his mouth
I wake him, "go to sleep" I say
His unfinished letter sits in front of him
A letter with a foreign structure to it
I recognize the writing but can't read it
When he writes he always writes in the same foreign language
Now I think, maybe, just maybe, he can't write in English

4.

Before he comes home he goes to the Orthodox temple in the neighborhood
Maybe he prays for his family to honor their deaths or prays for us
I want to think it's for us
I'm making all this up
I really don't know, all I know is
He goes every day and prays
I never wonder why   but today
Today I think he does it for reasons other than I know
It's awful to think I lived with this man
Now it feels as if this man isn't just a night watchman
Who cleans the laundry for his friend
So educated in so many languages,
He could or should or even was
A cantor, a rabbi,
He was never just my father who escaped the Nazis
He was I think   my father
But who was he really? just one of the survivors —
Who was Charlie Levin?
A man who lived in a country where no other Jews escaped
The only ghetto where operas were written and performed,
Where plays were written and performed
It was the only ghetto where a library was still in existence
When the war was over
The Jews left in the Vilnius ghetto
Were taken to the woods shot and killed; there were no survivors

5.

Questions burn today tomorrow
Take up residence in my dreams
Conversations play the piano
There is no one to ask
Today the music in my head
The words that leave my fingers determined and driven
These words I write live beyond knowing —
Who writes these words
Who is behind these poems
Who guides
Why now?

Why   a small word

Six brothers and sisters   lost to South Africa
Charlie number seven separates   lands in Chicago
Buried by a priest escapes

How now brown cow?

10 years rides the wind   never again
Seven brothers and sisters: strangers never again   a family

A Broken Woman

It's a gloomy dark day in the cemetery
It's funny I can't remember when
The dirt under my feet was this soft
My shoes sink   I watch the dirt lay over
I want to take my shoes off and stand barefoot
Squeeze soil between my toes
Say a real goodbye
Say I'll miss you

I see my breath as we all stand around
At my father's funeral
Without tears
Without conversation
We all stare in different directions

"It should be you!" I say in this ground in this wet
We don't talk for months after
5:30 a.m.   inhuman sounds shout through the phone
Hang-ups crying and more
I unlist my phone
I can't show any sympathy or be nice to her

"He's calling me!" she rants
Walking through the house
Always tearing at her hair
Endless hysteria: "No one loves me   I'm all alone
I gave up my life for you kids!"

One day while she cries out
she can't take it anymore
I finally say: "Why don't you
Eat that last piece of cheesecake you always leave on the
Kitchen table?"

The Grizzly Bear

The sound of the grizzly bear stomping through
The house

Moaning panting breathing heavy
Crying: "I'm hungry!"

She wears a helmet of fingers on her head

One thin slice of cheesecake sits on the
Kitchen table

She sleeps in a chair wearing a housedress
With the smell of yesterday

I Used to Play This Game with My Mother

She would throw knives forks spoons dishes

I would run and hide   singing at the top of my lungs:
"You can't catch me!"

The dining room table stands on a slant

She did catch me

Cheeks Hair Slamming Tables

"At least you don't have to sleep behind a locked door
You don't know how lucky you are —
You'll be sorry when I'm dead dead dead!

"I'll go outside and stand in the rain
I'll catch pneumonia then I'll die!
You'll be sorry!" — she always said that

One day when it was raining
I walk to the door and open it:
"Mother," I say "would you like to
Go stand in the rain?"
I laugh

She throws   *a plate*

Then I laugh again

She yells: "That's not funny!" pinches my cheek pulls my hair
And says: "I'll take pieces out of you!"

Lady Grizzly Roars

I open the door to a pitch-black room
From behind the door: a slap of rawhide
With a metal buckle smacks
Across my face

My legs come out from underneath —
The roar of the grizzly rages
From behind the door: insanity screams
My mother mumbles gibberish frantically

Without thinking my hands grab soft fatty flesh
I squeeze her arms till each of my fingers is stamped in blue

"It's midnight! Where have you been?"

I've been where all good children go
In a bar in a car chatting with this one and that
Tramps and *whores* and *tramps* and *whores*
Then to bed to bed to bed

She lives in her own hell
Where jealousy and resentment are eaten
For breakfast lunch and dinner
She's "sorry" she's "really sorry" she begs cries:
"Never again!"

Cries again   always the same   I've heard that before
I punish her   I ignore her   it drives her crazy

I don't speak to her   for weeks
She talks to me   I walk away pretend I don't hear her
I stick my nose up in the air close my eyes   and turn to the left

She Was Completely Broken

She cries asks me if I know what it feels like
To love someone to love someone
not my father
Who doesn't know you exist?

The Shirt

On my toes I thumb through racks of blouses
I do this all the time looking for something unusual
Something different something exciting something wonderful
When there before my eyes there it is right in front
Of me   the most amazing shirt I've ever seen
Jumping and grabbing at it

Finally my mother says: "what are you doing?"

I'm so excited I can't talk   *ooh! ooh!!*
"Get this get this down for me   *please*
Isn't this amazing! This   shirt *wow!!*
Look at this shirt   it's so special"

It's all white with red stitching on the cuffs
Around the   the one pocket on the left side with a brass button
The stitching trims the entire shape of the shirt
An A-line shape with two brass buttons   one on each side
Connecting tabs on the bottom
It has wide sleeves   I love the shape
A ribbed red cotton sweater V-insert turtleneck
With a zipper up the front and bat sleeves

On the floor kicking and screaming:
"I want that shirt!   I want that shirt!"

"Why do you like that shirt? Who wears a shirt like that?" my mother asks
"Who are you? Where did you come from? I don't know anyone like you
I don't know how I got you   Why do you have to be this way?
Why can't you be like your sister? like everyone else"

She always says things like *that*

I *love* my shirt
I wear it to bed that night

We Were Never Friends

A hummingbird sings on a bright sunny day
I could   never imagine   these words:

"We   were never   friends I want you   to know
I've always admired you   you're so strong
So determined never   let anything stop you
I could never do any of   those things
Be   as strong or determined"

She never knew words   words   like this:
"You and I have never   been friends"

A   hummingbird sings   from her bed
A song of goodbye a song   I could   not think   to think

After years of 5:30 a.m. rants   I unlist   my phone —
The phone call — the operator:
"There's an emergency   call your brother-in-law"

Now   I   stand by her bedside
My chestnut hair up in a twist   away from my face
Knee-length green-on-green   dress
With a cowl collar   three-quarter sleeves
Brown belt   pointed-toe Italian pumps

Numb   I must have been   numb confused stunned
Who's   in this bed? my mother never knew words like this
Where's   my mother?

I couldn't listen to her   I'll come back tomorrow
Insane rage   shock   I was in shock

This woman was not my mother   my mother never could say these words
She knew   something I didn't and left me with words
That only now I hear

I never saw her again   she flew away on the wind   I suppose

Nightmare   An Old Friend

1.

How many nightmares do you have?
How many have you buried?
How many times a night do you think you've
Heard the phone ring?
How many times do you wake thinking you've heard
The key in the door?
Do you ever sleep sound?
Do you ever have peace?

2.

"I remember the first time I saw him
He was so beautiful
He was fresh and new   a shiny penny

He has   your hands I said
Powerful strong hands   to build a future

I couldn't take my eyes off him
I couldn't look away"

3.

"Take a deep breath" I say
I watch   you exhale blow a ring of smoke
Listen to the sound   the tone of your words
Fixate on your mouth opening and   closing
While you chew   chew each word
Each word   blows its horn — an unforgettable note
Its rhythm repeats   your voice implying
What   is   *this*?   why does old friend nightmare —
Your life — live in mine?
Years go by without   without notice of gone or going
Or back again   and again and again

4.

Alone in the dark is a bad place; nightmares hide there   they wait
Wait for the opportune moment — one when the seasons change
Days turn dark early   winds howl turn umbrellas inside out
Late at night when all is quiet   the quiet just before a storm
Air so thick you can slice with a knife   a twist and shout of wind
A wind that bangs against   your sleep   shakes its fist
Hard   at your tomorrow — why even the dead   open their eyes!

Dearest

It's always a whole lot of rainbows
A whole lot of sunshine
After we've been away from one another
Many days and nights of summer rains
Thunderous lightning rods pierce   your love squeezes   my heart
Begging   so I give it

Warm days and nights full of humility   your touch you whisper
You're mine, I'll never never   never let you go

Fall leaves paint every color every emotion   expose my fear
My trust
Our bodies swim in green yellow rivers full of love rush us
Upstream —
Out into the ocean where this love swims for its life

Winter comes in with a cold breath   breathing in my ear
Down the back of my neck   my body shakes
You lay your storm over me
How to think   what to believe
There is no clue   no sound
Tomorrow   tomorrow is so far away

Dearest Love

There were so many cracks so many bad repairs
No way for success no way for the future to grow

I once looked into tomorrow:

You are always there
You always wear the same smile
Your arms stretch out to welcome me

I begin to want to walk towards you
Slow at first then the closer I get
The more frightened I become

The day is empty a gray sky
Where is the wind?
Where is the sun?
There is no air to breathe

You start to fade the closer I get
It rains
It thunders
Fires burn

Why is it always the same?
All those promises misspelled

Dearest Love

No one will ever love as much as I do

You squeeze our world till it disappears
Never let me forget   how lucky I am
We both know there is always a possibility
For the doorbell to ring

When the door opens our life could change forever
We will never have these moments again

What will you tell people?

Dearest Love

I love the way you love
Your love helps me live —
White clouds lie over our promises —
It protects us from the weather
Your music plays songs deafening
The static on the radio

Dearest

Promises promises more lies
A heart breaks in two
Squeezes breath a gasp for air
Toss turn chatter serves tea at 3:00 a.m.

You promise you promise   don't cherish betray
Don't hold us close let go and go
Lies expected they say they all say
You promise to stay true tell the truth

Bodies touch often words spill break apart more than once
Lies continue without fear
Weeks days a year   winter summer fall winter
Passion rises lies too   promise promise this promise
Fades away with a last kiss the kiss we kiss

We both walk away say goodbye
All promises lost somewhere — between our bed our lovers
Touch another and another   both keep secrets
Truth crawls in and out of dreams disturbs peace
Hides in the cracks of walls we live in
In our thoughts while we sleep in our dreams

We hold on by a string truth rings out comes between
Denial will keep my love the truth will destroy us

Love Poem

Eyes sparkle   fill a room with sun the day is magical
Gives a heart a reason to listen   the body is alive
It wants what it wants   words leave empty spaces without punctuation
Broken want   a sky turns dark   a lie leads the way
The spell is broken   the scar will run deep

Dearest Another Love

I stand in front of your painting
But it's really my design
You and I use the same technique
Concrete walls and color
Clothes that don't fit
Colors most won't wear

The clock is ticking
I listen to each second
The rhythm of my heart beats
It's for you of course
You're the only one I will ever love
I still want to dance with you
Across our lives across our broken promises

The notes you play
Are notes that help me
Want to open my eyes to tomorrow
To open my eyes to another bright sun
Or the rain or to sit by the phone

By the phone and wait just wait
I will wait for however long it takes
For you to dial   once I hear the tone
I'll know   it's a long time

Madly in Love

I wake with your body wrapped around mine

I feel safe
Cuddled up in the pit of your arm
I'm hiding from the day
I take a deep breath and breathe digest promises this   wanting

The morning has bright sun
Like the smile I wear   I don't want to untangle unlock or   let   go
It frightens me — I'm so happy
You whisper secrets to me   I'll keep forever
Bury them in a grave   of never to be told
I'm a great lover a bad friend

Your electric fingers   rub my skin
I feel fire run through my veins
The hair on my body stands up
I taste your lips   soft plump cushions   I sink into
Feel your breath on my face

Love your love   the way it fits   how we —
How it drapes over me like a well-fitted dress
A new skin perfect silk smooth
Waiting to be touched

Acknowledgments

The author extends her thanks to the following publications:

Poetry in Performance, 33
(City College of New
York/CUNY Press, 2005)

"We Were Never Friends"

Poetry in Performance, 38
(City College of New
York/CUNY Press, 2010)

"The Key"

First Literary Review — East,
May 2011

"I Used to Play This Game with My Mother"

*Spiny Babbler Arts of
Kathmandu Anthology*, eds.
Brant Lyon & Lisa Wolsky,
(Spiny Babbler, 2012)

"Fragments"

About the Author

Dividing livelihood between New York and Chicago may be all Ice Gayle Johnson does by half. The cool plurality of her sibilant first person suggests a lineage, an eponymous book title, perhaps, in itself — oracular. Empery, certainly, the lot of her talents — its salad of diversity, distribution and influence — decidedly Caesar, no mere lettuce. Already *multi*, media among her many hands further subsume boundary; evince *singular*, quite apart from uniqueness as poet, editor, publisher, performer, and photographer. Ice assays beauty vital in its combinatorial aesthetic, transformation and ascription to the *everyday*: the artist *complete*, recognizable as well to Warhol as Baudelaire.

The stylist, she shapes hair — sculpts, carves, clips, cuts, colors, configures and casts: supplements, creates — or, as case varies, complements — image everywhere we see. The "Five-point Cut," "Graduated Bob," and "Fire Fly" are hers. Former artistic director and general manager for Vidal Sassoon of Chicago, designer and developer of salons, teacher, consultant, *cicerone* of product and trend, she has sat on Clairol's Presidential Council side-by-side with Nancy Reagan's colorist, been juried into Intercoiffeur, and continues to maintain a cohort of private clients.

A founder and shaper of Uphook Press, Ice co-edited and contributed to its debut collection, *A Cautionary Tale: Peer into the Lives of Seven New York Performing Poets*, in 2008. Three other anthologies have followed: *you say. say.* (2009), *Hell Strung and Crooked* (2010), and *gape-seed* (2011).

Professional photographer, she has been represented by Ward Nasse Gallery, New York, participating in group shows from 2000 through 2006. Her photographs have been published by Marcel Schulman Greeting Cards, Signature Greetings, Broader Bond, and Greeting Card Software.

Ice the performance poet tours coast to coast — from the Bowery Poetry Club in New York to The Beat Museum in San Francisco. Her spoken word tracks have been featured by *Stay Thirsty Media* and Poetz.com. Eponymous CD and DVD are available at CDbaby and at DVD.com.

For more information about her multitude of goings on visit her website (that she of course designed and built) at www.icephotopoet.com.